DESERT WARFARE

by

Wallace B. Black
and
Jean F. Blashfield

CRESTWOOD HOUSE

New York

Maxwell Macmillan Canada
Toronto

Maxwell Macmillan International
New York Oxford Singapore Sydney

Library of Congress Cataloging-in-Publication Data

Black, Wallace B.
  Desert warfare / by Wallace B. Black and Jean F. Blashfield. —
1st ed.
      p.   cm. — (World War II 50th anniversary series)
  Includes index.
  Summary: Describes the strategies, battles, and ultimate effects of the
desert campaign against the Germans and Italians in North Africa during
World War II.
  ISBN 0-89686-561-4
  1. World War, 1939-1945 — Campaigns — Africa, North — Juvenile
literature. [1. World War, 1939-1945 — Campaigns — Africa, North.]
I. Blashfield, Jean F. II. Title. III. Series: Black, Wallace B.
World War II 50th anniversary series.
D766.82.B56 1992
940.54'23--dc20

91-27186
CIP
AC

JUVENILE
D
766.82
.B56
1992

Created and produced by B & B Publishing, Inc.

Picture Credits
Dave Conant, Map - page 35
Imperial War Museum - page 19
National Archives - pages 3, 5, 6, 7, 9, 10, 13, 14, 15, 17, 21, 22, 23, 25, 28, 31, 33, 39, 40, 45, 45

CRESTWOOD HOUSE

Macmillan Publishing Company
866 Third Avenue
New York, NY 10022

Maxwell Macmillan Canada, Inc.
1200 Eglinton Avenue East
Suite 200
Don Mills, Ontario M3C 3N1

Macmillan Publishing Company is part of the Maxwell Communication Group of Companies.

Printed in the United States of America

First Edition

10 9 8 7 6 5 4 3 2 1

CONTENTS

Chapter 1
ITALY — DISASTER IN AFRICA

It was September 13, 1940. Italian troops marched eastward from the Italian colony of Libya to attack British forces in Egypt. With flags waving and trumpets blaring, Italian Marshal Rodolfo Graziani led his invading army across the Libyan border into Egypt. The Italian dictator, Benito Mussolini, was intent on conquering this British-dominated country and throwing out the British.

Italy had been involved in African affairs since the 19th century when it assumed the protectorate of Somaliland. During the same period the British occupied an area adjacent to the northwest called British Somaliland. In 1912 Italy also took control of Libya on the Mediterranean Sea in North Africa. It was still an Italian colony at the beginning of World War II.

In 1935 the Italians decided to expand their presence in East Africa and invaded Ethiopia. The Duke of Aosta, a cousin of King Victor Emmanuel of Italy, was made viceroy of Ethiopia and ruled that country at the start of World War II. Together with Italian Somaliland and Eritrea, which lay just to the north, these three countries were called Italian East Africa. They were located on the horn of Africa, which is the easternmost tip of that huge continent. The Duke of Aosta was eventually made governor-general of all of Italian East Africa.

In 1939 and 1940 Mussolini and Italy had been forced to take a backseat to Adolf Hitler as the German army con-

Ethiopian cavalrymen armed with outdated weapons were no match for the invading Italian army in 1935.

quered many of the nations of Europe. Mussolini and Marshal Pietro Badoglio, chief of the Italian general staff, decided they would show Hitler and the rest of the world that Italy was also a great military power. Mussolini had dreams of creating a vast new Roman Empire in Africa. To carry out this dream, in June 1940 the Duke of Aosta was ordered to attack British possessions in northeast Africa. The Italians also occupied parts of two neighboring British colonies, Kenya and Anglo-Egyptian Sudan.

The Libyan Campaign

In eastern Africa the Italians met with complete success. In 1936 they had easily defeated the Ethiopian army and taken control of that country. In 1940 the British, busy defending their homeland and fighting the Germans in Europe, were unable to stop the Italian invasion of their East African colonies.

Flush with these victories, the Italian armies in Libya attacked across the Egyptian border. Marshal Graziani knew this would be no easy task, but following orders he sent his army charging into Egypt. Mussolini expected him to march 300 miles across Egypt to capture the giant British naval base at Alexandria. From there he was to capture Cairo, the capital of Egypt, and then take control of the Suez Canal. All this would take place across great distances

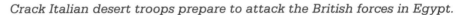

Crack Italian desert troops prepare to attack the British forces in Egypt.

Italian light tanks maneuvering in the Libyan desert

and against the smaller but well-equipped British army.

Led by Italian Blackshirt regiments, which were experienced and tested in battle, huge columns of Italian infantry, artillery, and tanks surged into Egypt. In the first few days they met little resistance. The Italians advanced over 50 miles to the east. There they captured a key airfield and a town called Sidi Barrani. However, reluctant to advance farther, Graziani set up a strong defensive position to defend against a British counterattack.

The attacking Italian regiments were leading the way for a huge force of over 250,000 men. The British had fewer than 100,000 to defend all of Egypt and its neighboring British colonies. In addition, the Italian navy and air force outnumbered the British. In the Mediterranean Sea the Italians had 75 warships and over 110 submarines. The British had only 33 warships and 12 submarines. The Italian air force could put over 300 aircraft into the attack on Egypt while the Royal Air Force (RAF) had only about 200 to defend against them.

Graziani knew that even though he had numerical superiority the British were better equipped and better trained. He decided to wait for a British counterattack before advancing farther. He had a defensive force of 80,000 men at Sidi Barrani waiting for an attack. The only action had been small battles along the Libyan-Egyptian border in which the Italians had suffered over 3,000 casualties while the British had only a few hundred killed or wounded.

The British Strike Back

Under the command of General Sir Archibald Wavell, the British were well equipped and ready to fight the invaders. As the Italians attacked, the British ground forces carried out a planned retreat into Egypt to set up a defense line at the town of Mersa Matruh. There they waited for reinforcements to arrive from India, New Zealand, Australia and Great Britain. Over 100,000 fresh troops would arrive in the next two months. In the meantime the Italians did nothing but reinforce their defenses.

The British Royal Navy was also reinforced during this period of inactivity in Egypt. On November 11, 1940, under the command of Admiral Sir Andrew Cunningham, ships and planes of the Royal Navy went on the offensive. That night planes from the aircraft carrier *Illustrious* attacked the harbor at Taranto, Italy. A large number of Italian warships lay at anchor there.

RAF Fairey Swordfish torpedo bombers swept in and sank one battleship and damaged two others. This action temporarily returned superiority at sea to Great Britain. British transport ships carrying reinforcements and supplies through the Mediterranean were now able to reach Egypt with relative ease.

On land early in November, General Wavell had learned that there was a large hole in the Italian defenses at Sidi

Italian troops advancing in an orderly column toward Egypt, confidant of a quick victory

Barrani. Using his recently reinforced ground troops, Wavell ordered an attack. On November 9 the newly arrived troops from India, Australia and New Zealand — in addition to British regulars — burst through the weak spot in the Italian defenses. They attacked and surrounded the surprised Italians and struck them from both front and rear. The Italian defenses crumbled and Graziani's Tenth Italian Army began a headlong retreat back into Libya.

Taking advantage of the successful surprise attack, the British army followed in hot pursuit. Armored troops led by tanks struck inland across the Libyan desert to cut off the Italians as they fled along the Mediterranean coast road. The RAF and the Royal Navy bombarded the Italians as they fled. Wavell's commander in the field, General Sir Richard O'Connor, led the main British force close behind the enemy. His men took Italian prisoners by the thousands as they tried to retreat.

The Italians continued this mad retreat for over 300 miles back into Libya. A force of only 30,000 British and colonial troops had routed the invading Italian army of 80,000. When this action was halted the first week of February 1941, the British forces had advanced almost 500 miles from their bases in Egypt. They overran additional towns and bases in Libya and trapped more Italians. The British captured over 130,000 Italians and more than 1,000 tanks and guns. It was a great victory for the British in which they suffered fewer than 2,000 casualties.

In Italian East Africa British forces were reinforced by South African air and ground forces. They quickly defeated the Italian forces there and took control of all of East Africa.

Italian forces leaving a damaged truck by the side of the road as they flee before the advancing British Eighth Army

Chapter 2

GERMAN ARMY TO THE RESCUE

All of North Africa lay open and waiting for the British to advance farther into Libya and beyond. If Wavell had been able to follow up on the victories scored in Libya, the Allies would have quickly gained control of all of North Africa and the Mediterranean Sea. But British troops, ships and aircraft were needed to fight the Nazis both at home and in Greece.

In 1939 Italy had invaded the tiny nation of Albania, which lies between Yugoslavia and Greece across the Adriatic Sea from Italy. The Albanians gave up without a fight. In October 1940 the Italians were still enjoying their early success in Egypt, when they decided to attack Greece. They launched a major attack from their bases in Albania. Mussolini was jealous of the many victories of Nazi Germany to the north. He wanted to prove to Hitler and the world that he too could conquer one country after another.

Although the Greeks had only a small and poorly equipped army, they were able to halt the Italian attack. The Italian forces did not have the strength or the leadership to fight a war in both Greece and North Africa at the same time. Defeated in Libya, the Italians were also defeated in Greece, first in November 1940 and then again in March 1941.

Honoring an earlier promise to help Greece if it were attacked, Prime Minister Winston Churchill of Great Britain ordered Wavell to send troops from Egypt. In November 1940 a small force of RAF fighters and bombers was sent to Greece to help drive the Italians back into Albania. But

Rommel turned the first German raids into a major advance. Although Hitler had ordered Rommel to remain on the defensive, the German general could not resist the opportunity to continue his offensive. Without regard for personal safety, Rommel flew over his advancing columns to direct each battle with the retreating British.

After only three weeks of battle, Rommel's Afrika Korps had driven the British back to the Egyptian border. By June 1941 Rommel had regained the entire 500 miles the Italians had lost. Outmaneuvered by the German tanks and their lightning armored attacks, the British retreated.

Rommel's supply lines were stretched to the limit. And the British navy and the RAF continually bombarded the coastal highway and prevented shipments of supplies from reaching the Germans by land. In addition the Ninth Australian Division held the major seaport at Tobruk, about 100 miles behind the farthest German advance. Although besieged by the Germans, the "Rats of Tobruk," as the British defenders called themselves, prevented the Afrika Korps from receiving supplies by sea at a point where they were most needed.

A German Luftwaffe Junkers JU-52 at a Libyan airfield. These slow transports were used to fly in troops and supplies.

High-speed and highly maneuverable armored cars used for reconnaissance by panzer divisions of the Afrika Korps

Rommel's first successful advance was stalled in Libya at the town of Bardia on the Egyptian border. Wavell counterattacked with newly reinforced British troops. Even with a shortage of fuel and ammunition and under heavy attack, Rommel held his advanced position. Under pressure from Churchill, Wavell launched a major attack against Rommel in mid-June. It failed, with the loss of 100 tanks. The excellent antitank tactics of the Germans stopped that effort. At that point Wavell was removed from command and replaced by General Sir Claude Auchinleck. General Rommel began preparing to start an offensive into Egypt.

Chapter 3

THE DESERT FOX

Erwin Rommel was born in Heidenheim, Germany, in 1891, and began his military training in 1910. He served in France and Italy during World War I and was awarded many honors for his bravery in battle. When World War II broke out he was a major general, and in 1940 he gained his first experience in tank warfare as commander of the Seventh Panzer Division. That year, during the battle for France, he proved his skill as a tank corps commander. Following the failure of the Italians in Libya, Hitler sent Rommel to Africa to become commander of the famed Afrika Korps.

In his first major action in Africa, Rommel scored one victory after another. Using surprise tactics and high-speed tank attacks, he outmaneuvered the British forces again and again. Flying over his advancing armored units in his private plane or joining them on the ground, he observed their progress firsthand. He seemed to be everywhere at once. His ability to outfox and outfight the British at every turn earned him the nickname Desert Fox.

The Second British Advance

Following the disaster in Greece, British forces in Egypt were steadily rebuilt. By November 1941 Auchinleck's forces had grown tremendously. He now commanded over 700 tanks, some 1,000 aircraft and over 100,000 troops. Facing him at the Libyan-Egyptian border, Rommel had a force only half that size. With four divisions still busy besieging Tobruk, the Desert Fox had to summon all of his

General Erwin Rommel, the Desert Fox, with a panzer group in Libya

skill as he faced a major offensive from a British force that was once again superior.

On November 18 the British launched the offensive called "Crusader." Striking inland, a large British armored force tried to do an end run to the south around the German defenders. At the same time the Rats of Tobruk launched an attempt to break through the German forces surrounding them.

Rommel immediately counterattacked and the battle seesawed back and forth for several weeks. Both sides suffered heavy losses of tanks and men. At first the Afrika Korps's superior desert warfare tactics were winning the battle. It appeared that Rommel's great ability as a leader would triumph. But short of supplies and with more and more tanks lost in battle, Rommel finally had to withdraw. The German and Italian forces retreated across Libya, giving up once again the more than 600 miles they had gained.

Rommel avoided the encircling British forces and set up a new defense line.

On December 31 he was back at the town of El Agheila where he had started nine months before. Tobruk had been relieved and the British once again controlled eastern Libya.

But Rommel, always the Desert Fox, had mastered the art of desert warfare. After conducting a successful retreat, the Afrika Korps was immediately resupplied with new tanks and fresh troops. Supplies were now reaching Rommel at a steady pace. The Luftwaffe and the Italian navy had defeated the British fleet and again regained control of the Mediterranean. By January 21, 1942, Rommel was ready to go on the offensive once again.

Rommel's Second Advance

On January 22 Rommel began his second major offensive and sent the British reeling backward. His newly reinforced Afrika Korps, now called the Panzer Army Africa, attacked to the northeast. In only 12 days Rommel's forces pushed the British back over 300 miles along the Mediterranean coast. On the way they captured the town of Benghazi and huge amounts of British supplies.

Meanwhile, other panzer units drove inland across the Libyan deserts. They overran British forces defending outlying forts and outposts along the way. These panzers joined the main German forces at the seaport town of Gazala.

The British put up a stiff defense where they had created the Gazala line, a series of strong points, or "boxes," each about two miles square. This line stretched about 40 miles inland from the coast. Each box was heavily defended by infantry and artillery. Over 700 tanks, including hundreds of the newly arrived American-made General Grant M3 tanks, supported the defensive boxes. A giant and well-armed force, the British Eighth Army, under the command of Major General Neil Ritchie, was preparing to stop the invading panzers at all points.

British Crusader tanks maneuver in preparation for the Battle of Gazala.

The Battle of Gazala

For the next several months both sides gathered their forces and made preparations for the next big battle. Rommel continually scouted the enemy positions by land and from the air. The British learned a great deal about the panzer army in the same manner and from intercepted German radio messages. On May 26, 1942, Rommel was ready to attack once again.

On the afternoon of that day, units of the Panzer Army Africa and several Italian army groups commanded by Lieutenant General Ludwig Cruewell attacked the northern boxes of the Gazala line. Because of the screaming Stuka dive-bombers of the Luftwaffe that were supporting the attack, the British thought this was the main attacking force. Tanks rushed from the rear to stop the attack. But the Desert Fox had fooled them.

Rommel had led his main forces around the southern end of the Gazala line at Bir Hacheim. That night and on the following day the German panzers bypassed the British defenders there. Rommel then led his lightning attack northward, defeating several large British armored forces on the way. The surprised British troops panicked and retreated toward Egypt. The goal of the German force was to cut off British communications and supplies and to attack the Gazala boxes from the rear.

The "Cauldron"

The main defensive box of the British side of the Gazala line was in an area that was to become known as the "cauldron." It was defended on the west by heavy minefields and on the other three sides by the 150th British Brigade Group and the First Army Tank Brigade. Forming a large circle about ten miles across, this courageous army fought off Rommel's repeated attacks. With the British forces to the north holding the line, the Panzer Army Africa had to break a path through the 150th Brigade. They needed to open a supply line for badly needed fuel for their tanks and ammunition for their guns.

The cauldron was so named because it became a boiling area of death and destruction for the defenders. The courageous British brigade held out for five days. Under continuous aerial bombardment and artillery attacks, they finally surrendered on June 1, 1942.

With his supply line now secure, Rommel turned his attention back to the defenders at Bir Hacheim to the south. Defended by a force of British and Free French troops, that outpost was a thorn in Rommel's side. The Free French forces were the French army units stationed in Africa that had not surrendered to the Germans after the fall of France. Rommel could not continue his advance northward while

Free French troops advancing during the battle at Bir Hacheim

Bir Hacheim was controlled by the British and the French. After wiping out the cauldron defenders, Rommel turned his full attention to the south. The brave British and Free French troops held out for ten days before abandoning the strategic fortress at Bir Hacheim.

Tobruk Finally Falls

By June 15 the last of the Gazala boxes had fallen. The German panzers were on the march toward Egypt once again. Rommel then turned his attention to the key city of Tobruk. A major seaport, Tobruk was defended by over 35,000 British troops, mostly from South Africa and other colonies. Huge quantities of supplies were stored there. Rommel insisted that it be taken before advancing farther.

In mid-June Tobruk came under direct attack by the Germans once again. During the first German advance in

1941, it had held out successfully for months. This time it fell in only a week. Heavily bombarded and cut off from help from the retreating British army, Tobruk surrendered. Although a huge amount of supplies had been destroyed by the defenders, an equally large amount was captured by the German attackers. Rommel now possessed another major seaport to receive reinforcements and supplies.

British Retreat to El Alamein

Following the fall of the Gazala line and Tobruk, General Auchinleck relieved General Ritchie and took over command of the Eighth Army himself. On June 25, 1942, the British retreated along the Mediterranean coast to Mersa Matruh and then to El Alamein. They had now been driven back 240 miles into Egypt. They were only 60 miles from the city of Alexandria on the Mediterranean. If Rommel's forces captured that key seaport, Egypt would be doomed and the Suez Canal would also fall under control of the Germans.

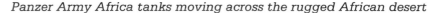

Panzer Army Africa tanks moving across the rugged African desert

British prisoners of war being driven behind the German lines after having been captured during the battle for the Gazala line

At El Alamein Auchinleck and the British forces dug in. For six weeks they successfully fought off the attacks of the Panzer Army Africa. The first battle of El Alamein was won by the British but with great cost in men and equipment. Following the major defeats at Gazala and Tobruk, and with continued heavy losses, it was decided that Auchinleck had to be replaced. In August new army commanders were brought to Egypt.

Churchill placed General Sir Harold Alexander in command of the British and Allied forces in the Middle East. Lieutenant General Bernard Montgomery was given command of the British Eighth Army. Their only goal was to go into the desert and defeat Rommel.

Chapter 4

MONTGOMERY TAKES CHARGE

The battles with Rommel, the Desert Fox, had been a disaster for the British Eighth Army. Tens of thousands of men were casualties or had surrendered. Hundreds of tanks and thousands of guns and vehicles of all sorts had been lost to the enemy. The morale of everyone — from private to general — was at rock bottom. But then came Monty. Lieutenant General Montgomery wanted his troops to call him by that nickname. To the misery of defeat he brought confidence. He stated, "From now on the Eighth Army will not yield a yard of ground to the enemy. Troops will fight and die where they stand."

From August 1942 to October 1942 British reinforcements poured into Egypt. They came from England through the Mediterranean Sea and from South Africa, India, New Zealand and Australia through the Suez Canal. Much-needed equipment and supplies came from the United States as well as from all of the British colonies. Thousands upon thousands of fresh troops arrived daily, along with tanks, big guns and support aircraft. Especially welcome were the mighty 36-ton Sherman tanks, with their 75mm cannon, fresh from factories in the United States.

Monty removed all thought or means of retreat. He threw away plans to defend Alexandria and the Suez Canal. Every activity and all training were aimed at preparation for the big offensive that was going to drive the Nazi army from Egypt. Gunners were drilled in antitank warfare. Tank crews and other mobile units were taught the skills of

General Bernard L. Montgomery watches his tanks move up shortly after taking command of the British Eighth Army.

desert warfare so bitterly learned. Monty demanded and obtained a high degree of discipline. In just 60 days a well-trained, spit-and-polish army was ready for battle.

Monty was not well liked by many of his officers. They resented his high-handed methods and his insistent demands for perfection. But they all looked up to him — and the enlisted troops loved him. They respected his will to win and his unwillingness to even think of defeat. He spoke their language. He told them that their job was to kill Germans and he was giving them the skills and the tools to do just that.

Rommel's Defeat at El Alamein

Rommel's Panzer Army Africa had set up a strong defensive line just to the west of El Alamein. Almost 40 miles long, the line started at the sea to the north and ended to the south at the Qattara Depression, rough and impassable desert country. Rommel knew that if the British Eighth Army were to attack, it would have to fight through his deep minefields and heavy defenses. There was no way to bypass or outflank his well-prepared and dug-in defenses.

But Rommel was not one to wait for the enemy to attack. Planning to break through the British lines and head for Alexandria, he ordered an attack on August 30, 1942. His plan called for a large force, including crack panzer divisions, to break through the British lines just north of the Qattara Depression. From there they were to drive north, cutting off the British forces from their headquarters and supplies.

But Monty was ready for the attack. Heavy minefields awaited the panzers and delayed their advance. And as Rommel headed his troops north they were stopped at Alam Halfa ridge. This strong point was located about ten miles behind the British lines and ten miles from the sea. There the Panzer Army Africa was met by deadly fire from carefully dug-in new Sherman tanks and heavy artillery. German tanks and other mobile units were destroyed.

After several days of heavy bombardment both from ground forces and from the RAF, Rommel's troops were forced to retreat. After losing some 50 tanks and suffering heavy casualties, Rommel's previously victorious army withdrew.

Monty Prepares to Attack

In spite of pressure from Churchill and other British leaders, Montgomery would not order an attack until he knew his army was ready. Too many of his men had just arrived and needed more training. Night and day he taught his troops desert warfare and trained them in the tactics needed to defeat the enemy.

Monty was a master of deception. His plan was to attack Rommel's forces at their strongest point near the north end of their defense line. While building up his forces in readiness to the north, he had a mock army built far to the south. Dummy tanks, soldiers and fake equipment in huge quantities were real enough to fool the Germans. They were certain that an attack would come from that direction.

Finally, as October drew to a close, all was ready. The British outnumbered the Germans by two to one in almost every category of troops and equipment. And the Germans were far from their sources of supply and had less than enough fuel and ammunition on hand to fight an extended battle. The Eighth Army, on the other hand, was well equipped and had ample supplies and reserves.

A final blow to German preparedness was the fact that Rommel, the Desert Fox himself, was seriously ill. He had been flown back to Europe for treatment. General George Stumme, who had served in Russia, was brought in to take Rommel's place. Under the circumstances it was an impossible task.

The British Attack Begins

At approximately 9:30 on the evening of October 23, 1942, the carefully planned British attack began. Bombs dropped on the unsuspecting Germans as hundreds of RAF bombers released their deadly cargo. Several thousand guns rained artillery shells on German targets at the rate of almost 1,000 a minute. It was the largest Allied artillery barrage of the war.

To the south, British forces launched a minor attack to carry out the idea that the main attack would come there. But to the north Monty's troops were starting to move forward under the protection of the gigantic aerial and artillery bombardment.

Speedy Stuart M3 tanks race toward the enemy.

Minefields were cleared and British troops poured across the no-man's-land approaching the German lines. The heavy bombing and shelling had taken a terrible toll on the Panzer Army Africa, but they were still able to fight back. Their commander, General Stumme, died of a heart attack early in the battle. But the well-disciplined and experienced German forces continued the battle. A physically ill Rommel arrived back from Europe on October 25 to take command once again.

Suffering one defeat after another and short of supplies, Rommel asked Hitler for permission to withdraw. Hitler refused and ordered him to stand fast and fight. Finally, with complete annihilation near, Hitler gave permission for the Panzer Army Africa to withdraw into Libya. With the Eighth Army close behind, the once mighty German panzers began a retreat that would not end until two months later when they reached Mareth, Tunisia, 1,200 miles to the west.

Chapter 5

OPERATION TORCH

Following the Japanese attack on Pearl Harbor on December 7, 1941, the United States declared war on Japan, Germany and Italy. Together they became known as the Axis powers. The United States immediately entered the war as an ally of Great Britain and prepared for action on all fronts. Many members of the armed forces of conquered European countries had escaped capture. They joined with British and American forces to help form a strong Allied military presence to fight the Axis.

Far to the north, Russia was under continuous attack by the German army. The Russian dictator, Josef Stalin, wanted the Allies to attack the German armies in Europe. This would take the pressure off the Russians. President Franklin Delano Roosevelt of the United States also insisted that American forces attack German-held territory.

In spite of these urgings, the Allied high command decided that an invasion of North Africa should come first. Called Operation Torch, the African invasion by Allied forces would help the battered Russians by pulling German troops away from the eastern front. It would also make possible the final defeat of Rommel's Panzer Army Africa. And a victory in Africa would provide the bases from which an invasion of Sicily and Italy would be launched.

A huge invasion fleet of almost 700 merchant vessels and warships was assembled during October 1942. This invasion fleet was at sea awaiting orders for Operation Torch to begin. On November 8, 1942, British-American forces landed in strength at three separate locations in North Africa. This giant force was commanded by the famous American general and future president Dwight D. Eisenhower.

That day American troops landed near Casablanca in French Morocco on the Atlantic coast of northwest Africa. At the same time two other large invasion forces made up of both British and American troops landed in Algeria on the north coast of Africa.

Hitler and the German high command had not expected this huge invasion. They were busy fighting the Russians far to the north. And in Africa they were busy trying to support Rommel as he retreated westward from El Alamein. When the Nazis finally realized that Operation Torch was under way it was too late. There was nothing the Germans could do to stop the huge American and British invasion called Torch.

French Forces in Africa — Friend or Foe?

Both Morocco and Algeria in North Africa were controlled by Vichy French forces. The Vichy French government had been established at the city of Vichy, France, by the Germans. Its task was to control unoccupied southern France and the French colonies in Africa for the Germans. The French in North Africa were bitterly divided. Many wanted to fight the Germans any way they could. Others were afraid to fight because to do so would bring immediate German occupation of all of southern France and French North Africa. They also feared German reprisals against the captive French people on mainland Europe.

The Allied command, however, figured that the French in North Africa would support the Allied invasion. They were only partly correct. Some French forces did support the American and British invading forces. Others just stood

A French warship disabled by its crew at a North African port following the British-American invasion

aside and did nothing. And still others actively fought the invasion. Eventually all French forces either laid down their arms or joined forces with the Allied armies under General Eisenhower.

As fighting with the French ceased, Admiral Jean-Francois Darlan, the French commander in North Africa, ordered the French fleet put out of action so that it would not be used by either the Allies or the Germans. Over 50 French warships were sunk. But Darlan did place the French army under the command of General Eisenhower.

The delay caused by the French forces was costly. The landing schedule had been slowed by almost a week. During that short period of time the Germans had been reinforcing their troops in Tunisia. They were ready to fight the Allies to the bitter end for North Africa.

The German Bridgehead in Tunisia

American and British troops had stormed ashore with great success at Casablanca in Morocco and at Oran and Algiers in Algeria. But while the invaders were being held up by the confused French resistance, fresh German and Italian troops were flown in from southern Italy. By the time Darlan had ordered the French to stop fighting, over 15,000 fresh Axis troops had landed in Tunisia.

The heavily protected and well-supplied German and Italian bases at Bizerte and the city of Tunis in Tunisia were only 100 miles from the Italian island of Sicily. Easily supplied by air and sea, the Germans and the Italians were once again preparing for battle.

At the same time Rommel, the Desert Fox, was leading his defeated forces westward along the coast of Libya. Rommel's retreating army, followed closely by the British Eighth Army, was speeding toward Tunis. Rommel wanted to join with the newly arrived Nazi forces there to attack the inexperienced American troops. Under the command of General Hans-Jurgen von Arnim, the German-Italian forces at Bizerte and Tunis soon numbered over 65,000, with new tanks and greatly reinforced units of the Luftwaffe.

The Casablanca Conference

By January 1943 the combined American, British and French forces were in place in North Africa. But the question of leadership was a problem with forces of three nations trying to fight a war together. There were bitter rivalries among the French generals. Many of the French hated the British, which made cooperation difficult. A single unified command needed to be established. And the huge American army was still untested in battle and in need of further training.

President Franklin D. Roosevelt and Britain's Prime Minister Winston Churchill met at Casablanca in Morocco in

A combined American and British force landing in Algeria during Operation Torch

January 1943. There they made plans for fighting the Germans and Italians in Europe and the Japanese in the Pacific theater. At that conference they brought the French rivals together and established firm policies of command in North Africa.

With General Eisenhower as supreme commander in North Africa, it was agreed that only one commander would be responsible for any army, navy or air force action involving combined forces of the three Allies. Eisenhower was ordered to proceed with the conquest of North Africa in preparation for an invasion of Italy.

Chapter 6

THE RACE FOR TUNIS

Following the successful landings in Morocco and Algeria, the Allied forces raced eastward into Tunisia. By January 1, 1943, advancing by land, sea and air, the American, British and French forces were in position along the Algerian-Tunisian border. They were less than 100 miles from the German bridgehead at Bizerte and Tunis. Although slowed by winter rain and muddy roads, they had advanced steadily.

The two opposing armies were separated by several mountain ranges, including the Western Dorsal and the Eastern Dorsal. The German-Italian forces were in position between the eastern range and the Mediterranean Sea. They were making preparations not only to defend their bridgehead but also to attack the inexperienced American troops. By early February they had two major armies on the Tunisian coastal plain — General von Arnim's Fifth Army and Rommel's Panzer Army Africa, which had arrived at Mareth, Tunisia, 200 miles to the south. Using old French fortifications Rommel had set up defenses, called the Mareth line.

The Luftwaffe and Panzers Attack

As the green American troops advanced they were bombed continuously by the Luftwaffe. Having achieved temporary air superiority, German Stuka dive-bombers rained bombs on advancing American and French army

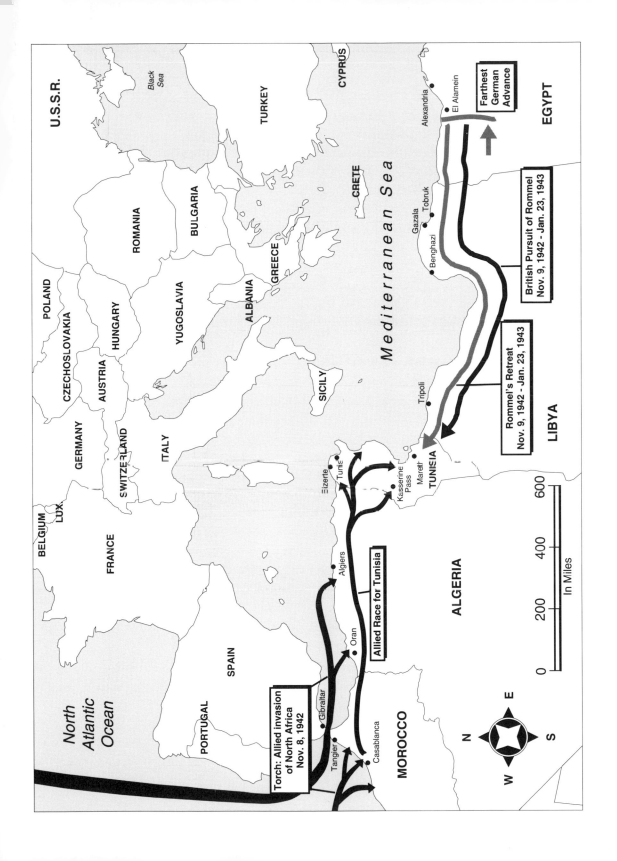

units along the coastal highways of Algeria and Tunisia. In spite of the fierce German attacks, however, the Allied forces had reached the Eastern Dorsal mountain range and were within striking distance of Bizerte and Tunis.

On January 18, 1943, General von Arnim unleashed a major attack against the most advanced Allied forces. Led by a large infantry and tank force known as *Gruppe Weber*, the panzers and Stukas drove back the French forces that were leading the Allied advance. Counterattacks by the American XIX Corps slowed the German attacks. Even so, the Allies were forced to retreat to the Western Dorsals, giving up much valuable territory to the Germans. But the Allied forces moved eastward again, preparing to attack the German Tunisian bridgehead.

Rommel Returns to Battle

Rommel's Panzer Army Africa had raced westward toward Tunisia in retreat from El Alamein. They reached the town of Mareth in southeast Tunisia on January 23, 1943. Poorly equipped after the 1,400-mile retreat, Rommel's army was soon reinforced. Several Italian and German divisions joined the panzer army and were stationed on the Mareth line to hold back the advancing British Eighth Army, which had pursued them all the way from Egypt.

The Desert Fox, working closely with von Arnim, prepared two well-equipped panzer army groups. Two divisions were to cut through the center section of the Eastern Dorsal range at the city of Faid. They were to attack and capture the key village of Sidi Bou Zid and the Kasserine Pass located in the Western Dorsal. Rommel himself led an Italian division and his own Afrika Korps on an end run to the south of the mountain range to attack the same two targets.

Chapter 7

THE BATTLE OF KASSERINE PASS

By mid-February 1943 the Allied armies outnumbered the Axis forces in almost every category. But the American II Corps, stationed on the southwestern slopes of the Eastern Dorsals, was not at all ready for a major battle. Badly commanded by Major General Lloyd R. Fredendall, the II Corps had not properly prepared its defenses and reserves were poorly positioned.

The combined French and American XIX Corps was stationed at the center of the Allied defense line. Although eager for battle they were badly equipped with much of the same type of arms and equipment they had used when they lost the battle for France in 1940. The northern sector, along the Mediterranean, was manned by the British forces. They were well equipped and ready to fight.

The German attack was unleashed on February 14. Von Arnim's forces, attacking as planned, burst through the mountain pass at Faid. Rommel's forces met with equal success as they drove northward to join von Arnim for the attack on the Kasserine Pass. Screaming Stuka dive-bombers supporting roaring panzers gave the American soldiers their first real taste of blitzkrieg warfare. The American and French forces were driven back as far as 40 miles all along the central Tunisian front with heavy casualties. A hundred or more tanks were lost and thousands of Americans were killed, wounded or captured.

Numerous American units were trapped and surrounded by the attacking panzers. Others, facing a superior enemy for the first time, retreated in panic. Rescue missions and counterattacks were attempted, but all failed. The battle-torn units of the American II Corps fled before the German panzers and supporting infantry. The Panzer Army Afrika was ready to attack the Kasserine Pass and drive through onto the plains of Algeria.

A Costly German Delay

The Americans had little chance of stopping the Germans at the pass. They had been defeated and forced to retreat with every German attack. In just two days' time the victorious German battalions were approaching Kasserine from both the east and the south. This key pass through the Western Dorsals was the gateway to Algeria and the Allied bases and airfields that lay just beyond the Western Dorsals.

But von Arnim and Rommel could not agree on a plan of attack. Von Arnim insisted on waiting for orders from their commander, Field Marshal Albert Kesselring, who had his headquarters in Italy. Rommel wanted to take advantage of their battlefield successes and continue the attack at once. His plan called for charging through the Kasserine Pass and then westward to capture the key town of Tebessa. Two days were lost before he received instructions to continue the attack.

On February 19, 1943, Rommel's forces attacked Kasserine Pass. American infantry, artillery and tank de-stroyers set up a defense to trap the German panzers in the pass. Despite severe losses the ill-trained American defenders held on. Reinforcements arrived, and following a day and night of fighting, they kept the advancing panzers bottled up in the Kasserine Pass. But not for long. On February 20, American resistance was shattered. Axis tanks and infantry poured through the pass onto the plains to the west. There was no opposition on the road to Tebessa or

American and British reinforcements were rushed eastward from Algeria to support the battles in Tunisia.

the road northward to Thala and the Algerian coastline.

But, for a change, Rommel became overly cautious, fearing a counterattack by the Americans and the British. He wanted to gather his forces and prepare to fight off the expected attack. Meanwhile, Allied reinforcements did arrive and set up lines of defense to the west and to the north. When the German attack was resumed, Rommel found the road to the west heavily defended. He ordered an attack on Thala to the north.

Allied Unlimited Resources Prevail

While the Kasserine Pass battle was under way, the Allies were rushing in men, tanks, artillery and supplies from as far away as Morocco and Algeria. Newly arrived guns and tanks took up positions to meet the German advance at Thala. After suffering heavy battle damage from gigantic artillery barrages, Rommel called off the attack. Short of supplies and still a sick man, Rommel ordered a retreat and led his previously victorious army back through the Kasserine Pass toward the Bizerte and Tunis bridgehead. The advancing Allied reinforcements followed close behind and once again set up a new line of attack along the Eastern Dorsal range.

To meet a new threat from the east, Rommel's force returned to the Mareth line. Montgomery and the British Eighth Army were ready to drive toward Tunis. To stop an attack before it began, Rommel's panzers launched an offensive action against the advancing British. But forewarned by excellent reconnaissance, British antitank units had laid a trap. Firing from hidden strong points, the British destroyed over 50 panzers in that first attack.

That was the end of Rommel in his role of the Desert Fox. His famed panzers retreated toward Tunis as the Mareth line was shattered. A few days later Montgomery's Eighth Army circled inland to join forces with the Allied forces advancing from the west. The Allied armies now had von Arnim's German and Italian army encircled and forced into a small northeast corner of Tunisia.

Change of Command

Sick with jaundice and other ailments, Rommel returned to Germany to consult with Hitler. The German dictator relieved Rommel of his command and appointed von Arnim commander of the newly formed Army Group Africa in Tunisia.

On the Allied side, the American general Fredendall had proved a failure. In the American II Corps alone the Allies had lost over 7,000 men and 250 tanks and guns. Because

General Patton (at left) coming ashore in Tunisia to assume command of the American II Corps

his unit commanders and troops had lost confidence in him, General Fredendall was relieved of his command. On March 6, another flamboyant warrior, General George S. Patton, appeared on the scene to take command of the American forces in the final battle for Tunisia.

Chapter 8

HILL 609
AND VICTORY

The battered German Army Group Africa withdrew farther into the Bizerte-Tunis pocket. Following the defeat at the Mareth line, fierce battles were fought between General Patton's II Corps and the retreating panzers. By the end of March, Montgomery's Eighth Army and its New Zealand Corps had driven north and joined up with Patton's advance units. Attacked on two sides, the remains of the once-great Afrika Korps retreated to the coast and north toward Tunis.

Allies Gain Air Superiority

As the land battle seesawed, the Allies were pushing the Axis forces deeper into their Bizerte-Tunis pocket. New American tanks and aircraft were being brought into the battle daily. Under the command of Air Marshal Sir Arthur W. Tedder, the RAF and the United States Army Air Corps drove the Luftwaffe from the skies over Tunisia. Together with the Allied navy, they destroyed hundreds of German and Italian ships and planes as they tried to bring reinforcements and supplies to the besieged German and Italian army.

Eisenhower had made British General Alexander commander of the ground forces in the final Tunisian campaign. Patton commanded the American II Corps. A tough disciplinarian, Patton whipped the previously beaten American troops into shape. While the British Eighth Army advanced

A U.S. Ranger battalion advances over rugged hills during the final days of the battle for Tunis.

past the Mareth line from the south, Patton's II Corps was attacking key targets in the north.

The Fall of Hill 609

The final German defense line was less than 50 miles from Bizerte and Tunis. But it was heavily defended, with Italian and German troops firmly entrenched on high hills. The northern fringes of the Dorsal mountain chains provided excellent defensive terrain for the German and Italian troops remaining. With artillery and machine guns mounted on the hills, the Axis gunners could fire down on the advancing Allies with deadly accuracy. The hills had to be taken.

Hill Djebel Fatnassas, Longstop Hill, the rugged hills and gullies of the Medjerda River and the giant Hill 609 were barriers that had to be attacked and overcome. Advancing Allied troops were being held up, and they suffered heavy casualties as they tried to move past the heavily defended high ground.

At the far north end of the German defenses stood Hill 609. Located on the main route to Tunis, it was 609 meters high — almost 2,000 feet — and was heavily defended. The Allied forces could not bypass Hill 609 without suffering heavy casualties. On April 30, 1943, General Omar N. Bradley, another famous American military leader, decided a direct attack was called for. He launched a heavy tank attack up the steep sides of Hill 609, leading the way for an infantry assault. This direct attack was successful and opened the way for the final drive to Bizerte and Tunis.

The Axis Surrounded by Land and Sea

By the first week of May 1943, the relentless attacks of the American II Corps and the British First and Eighth armies scored stunning victories daily. At sea the Royal Navy, under the command of Admiral Sir Andrew Cunningham, controlled the sea-lanes between Tunisia and Italy. Over 3,000 Allied aircraft were pounding the enemy from the air. The Axis troops were trapped and had no way to escape the Allied onslaught.

On May 6, following a heavy artillery barrage by more than 600 guns, the American and British troops found no resistance as they charged toward the Mediterranean coast. Enemy units were beginning to surrender on all sides. General von Arnim, however, led the remnants of his army out onto the Cape Bon peninsula below Tunis. Although ordered by Hitler to fight to the death, the proud German general finally surrendered when his panzer divisions ran out of fuel and ammunition.

Huge quantities of weapons such as this M-10 tank destroyer poured ashore in North Africa to hasten the defeat of the Axis forces.

On May 13, 1943, the war in North Africa was over. In an extended North African campaign that had lasted for more than three years, Axis armies totaling over 600,000 men had been destroyed. The Allies suffered over 260,000 casualties during the same period. In the Tunisian campaign alone over 250,000 German and Italian troops were captured and over 40,000 killed. The Allied casualties in this final campaign were fewer than 70,000.

The desert war was over. The way was now clear for the Allies to begin the invasion of Italy.

GLOSSARY

airborne troops Military units that are delivered to a combat zone by troop carriers, gliders or parachutes.

aircraft carrier A flat-topped ship on which aircraft take off and land.

Allies The nations that joined together during World War II to defeat Germany, Japan and Italy; France, Great Britain, the Soviet Union and the United States.

amphibious troops Ground troops that are delivered to a combat zone by troopships and landing craft.

antitank Refers to weapons, equipment or tactics used in fighting against tanks.

armor Refers to tanks and other armored vehicles used by an army.

artillery Land weapons such as cannon, howitzers and missile launchers suitably mounted and fired by a crew.

Axis The partnership of Germany, Italy and Japan during World War II.

barrage Heavy artillery fire placed in front of friendly troops to shield and protect them.

battleship The largest modern warship.

blitzkrieg Means "lightning war" in German.

bridgehead A fortified position established by a military force on one side of a body of water.

dive-bomber An aircraft designed to aim and release a bomb toward a target while in a nearly vertical dive.

infantry Foot soldiers in an army.

Luftwaffe The German air force.

minefield An area in which explosive mines have been placed underwater or buried on land.

Nazi A member of the National Socialist party that ruled Germany from 1933 to 1945 under Adolf Hitler.

panzer A German tank.

RAF The Royal Air Force of Great Britain.

tank An enclosed, armored combat vehicle armed with cannon and machine guns, that travels on caterpillar treads.

torpedo bomber An aircraft designed to carry bombs and launch torpedoes.

INDEX